Picture Sorting for Phonemic Awareness

by Nancy Jolson Leber

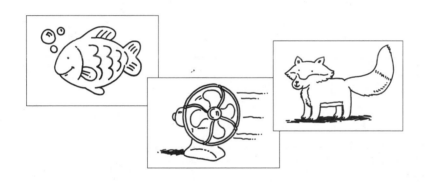

SCHOLASTIC
PROFESSIONAL BOOKS

NEW YORK • TORONTO • LONDON • AUCKLAND • SYDNEY
MEXICO CITY • NEW DELHI • HONG KONG • BUENOS AIRES

DEDICATION

To Rich—For your understanding about the piles of papers and books all over the floor,
and your patience with my late night and weekend work.

ACKNOWLEDGMENTS

Many thanks to Louisa Moats and Wiley Blevins
for their phonemic awareness expertise.

Cover design by Jim Sarfati
Cover illustration by Jane Dippold
Interior design by Solutions by Design, Inc.
Interior illustrations by Maxie Chambliss, Jane Dippold, Rusty Fletcher, James Graham Hale, and Ruth Linstromberg

ISBN: 0-439-28231-4

10   40   11/0

Contents

Introduction

Welcome to *Picture Sorting for Phonemic Awareness*! Designed especially for pre-readers, these easy hands-on activities and games help children develop an awareness of sounds, which is essential to reading success. Children examine picture cards, say the names of the pictures aloud, and sort the cards by how the words sound—for example, words that rhyme or begin with the same sound. The active process of sorting allows children to focus on specific word elements, such as onsets (initial sounds) or rimes (word endings). It encourages children to use higher-level thinking skills as they make generalizations, recognize the similarities and differences among words, and discover how words are related. Picture sorting is also a great way to reinforce content-area vocabulary. This book includes dozens and dozens of reproducible picture cards for sorting, as well as assessment ideas and games—everything you need for lots of picture-sorting fun!

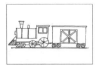

What Is Phonemic Awareness?

Phonemic awareness is the ability to hear, identify, and manipulate the separate sounds, or phonemes, that make up words. Speech can be analyzed into separate words, words can be broken down into syllables, and syllables can be broken down into separate units of sounds, called phonemes. For example, the word *pig* has three phonemes: /p/, /i/, and /g/. By changing the first phoneme in *pig* from /p/ to /b/, the word changes to *big* and, of course, the meaning changes as well. Helping children develop an awareness of phonemes and the ability to manipulate them is an essential step in emergent literacy instruction.

Phonological awareness is a broader term that includes phonemic awareness and also encompasses an understanding of syllables, onsets and rimes, alliteration, rhymes, and words. It is the ability to attend to the sounds of spoken words rather than their meanings. Decades of research highlight the importance of phonological awareness for beginning readers. In fact, studies have identified phonological awareness and letter knowledge as the greatest contributors to reading success. Children who can analyze the sounds of spoken words are more successful in learning to read printed words.

Getting Started

The activities in this book help young children build skills in recognizing rhymes, matching beginning sounds, counting syllables, and counting phonemes. Each of the picture-sorting sections in this book lays the groundwork for the next, but the sections do not need to be followed in sequence. You may use them in the order presented here or in a different order to meet children's needs.

On each reproducible page, you'll find two sets of picture cards to be used together in a sorting activity. The names of the pictures appear at the bottom of the page for the teacher's reference. In advance, cut apart the cards. Review the picture names with children before they begin sorting. Then have children sort the cards into two groups. To customize learning, have children sort two sets of cards from different pages. For a greater challenge, have them sort more than two sets of cards.

Picture Sorting for Phonemic Awareness   Scholastic Professional Books

Within each section, the picture cards are arranged in order of difficulty. The sets of cards at the beginning of each section provide the most obvious contrasts. Throughout the section, the sets progress to finer contrasts that present a greater challenge. At the beginning of the rhyming section, for example, children sort words that end in –at and –ice. At the end of the section, they sort words that end in –ock and –op, a more difficult task because the rimes both begin with the short o sound.

For greater durability, laminate the cards (you might color them before laminating). Store the cards in an envelope labeled with the target sound (such as -ing) or feature (such as 2 syllables). If you want to expand your picture-card collection, create additional cards by drawing pictures or cutting out pictures of familiar objects from old workbooks, magazines, or catalogs. Paste them onto unlined index cards or onto the blank cards on page 61. See page 62 for a list of additional picture words that can be used to expand your card collection. You might even start a collection of small objects and toys, such as plastic fruit, animal figurines, and dollhouse accessories, for children to sort by name.

How to Sort

To sort picture cards, children compare and contrast how words sound. They start by saying aloud the whole word, then focus on specific elements of words, such as onsets or rimes. Finally, children group together words that share a common element, such as the same number of syllables.

Use the same routine each time you introduce a sorting activity so children become familiar with the procedure. After you model the activity, have children sort a group of cards as you observe and guide them. When you feel children understand the process, have them sort independently or with partners. Below is a step-by-step description to take you through the process.

1 First, review the picture names and target sounds or features with children. In advance, choose a page of picture cards that you would like children to sort. Make a copy for each child and one for the demonstration. Cut apart the cards in advance. It is a good idea to start with the first page of cards in each section, since these are the easiest to sort. Choose one card from each set on the page as the key picture card. (Suggestions appear on page 62.) Identify the picture name and the target sound. For example, show children the cards for mug and sun and tell them: "Mug…mmmug begins with the sound /m/. Sun…sssun begins with the sound /s/." Present the rest of the picture cards and review the names of each. (Names appear at the bottom of each reproducible picture-card page.) Discuss the meaning of picture names as needed.

2 Next, model the sorting process with a few more cards. For example, tell children to listen to the beginning sounds in each picture name and decide if it sounds like /m/ as in mug. Demonstrate by thinking aloud: "This is a picture of a mop. Mmmop begins with the same sound as mug— /m/—so I'll put it below the picture of the mug."

Or for rhyming picture cards, tell children to listen for the ending sounds in each picture name and decide if they sound like *-at* as in *hat*. Demonstrate by exaggerating the sounds in each word: "This is a picture of a cat. *Caaat, haaat. Cat* has the same ending sounds as *hat, -at,* so I'll put it below the picture of the hat."

TEACHER TIP

Choose sets of cards for children to sort based on words or target sounds that they have recently come across in a book or class discussion.

3 Give children their own sets of cards to sort during guided practice. (Cut apart the cards in advance.) Have children say the picture names as you help them sort. Provide picture names if children can't identify them. Once children have sorted the cards, remove any whose picture names children can't remember. Then have children shuffle the cards and sort again, naming each picture aloud.

4 Finally, have children work with partners or independently to sort the cards into the same categories as above. When they are finished, ask children why they grouped together the cards as they did. Have children tell how the picture words in each group are alike. Guide children to identify the target sound that the words have in common.

TEACHER TIPS

For practice with oddity tasks, use one set of cards that all share the same target sound. Add one distractor (a picture name that does not feature the target sound). Include additional distractors to increase difficulty. Ask children to determine which card(s) do not belong with the rest and why.

For closed sorts, have children sort cards into categories that you have specified. For open sorts, have children examine a set of cards and sort them into categories of their own choosing.

Meeting Individual Needs

Tailor sorting activities to meet children's needs by adjusting the number of categories. Start with two categories of obvious contrasts. Increase the number of picture cards as children become more proficient. Eventually add a third or even fourth category to present a greater challenge. At the beginning of each section, you'll find additional ways to vary the activities in order to meet individual needs. You may also use the games on pages 52–60 to provide children with an extra challenge or additional practice.

To provide further reinforcement, read aloud rhymes and poems to small groups of children who need more practice. Have children raise their hand each time you say a word that features the target sound. You might also read aloud big books. Track the print as you read to help children build an association between the target sound and the corresponding letter(s).

Picture sorts are also ideal for first- and second-graders with limited reading vocabularies, English Language Learners (ELL), and children with special needs. To teach ELL children or to reinforce content-area vocabulary, children can sort pictures by categories, such as food, clothing, and animals.

TEACHER TIP

Before children begin a sorting activity, review the name of each picture with them. Have children say the names on their own to ensure that they know them.

Picture Sorting for Phonemic Awareness   Scholastic Professional Books

Working With Groups

The sorting activities in this book can be used with individuals, pairs, small groups, or the whole class. For whole-group instruction, photocopy the picture cards onto a transparency to use with an overhead projector. Or enlarge the cards on a photocopying machine and color them to use in a pocket chart. You might also use removable adhesive on the back of each card to affix it to the wall or chalkboard. When working with small groups, lay the cards faceup on the floor or on a table and gather children around so they all can see.

TEACHER TIPS...........................

Build on previous knowledge to help children experience success. For example, contrast a new target sound with a sound children already know.

Read rhyming or alliterative stories to improve children's sensitivity to sounds. (For suggestions, see the book list on page 63).
....

Assessing Students' Skills

Children acquire word knowledge through instruction. Since young children differ in their phonological awareness, determine each child's ability before beginning instruction and practice. Use the reproducible assessments at the beginning of each section of picture cards to determine children's levels of phonological awareness. Although individual assessment is preferable, you can also assess small groups of children at the same time (two or three children for pre-kindergarten and up to six children for kindergarten).

To begin, choose sorting activities that match children's developmental levels. If children are having difficulty sorting, have them sort each group of cards until they have mastered it before moving on to the next group of cards. Children are ready to move on to a new sorting activity when they can sort quickly and accurately.

The Five-Day Plan

It is ideal to have children work on picture sorting (or other phonological awareness activities) five days a week for 15 to 20 minutes per day. Refer to pages 8–9 for a five-day plan. The five-day routine can be modified for three days a week as described below.

Day 1
(Days 1 and 2 of the five-day plan)
Model/Guided Practice
Sort Again/Color (as independent practice)

Day 2
(Days 3 and 4 of the five-day plan)
Draw
Search for Pictures (as independent practice)

Day 3
(Day 5 of the five-day plan)
Games

The Five-Day Plan

MODEL/GUIDED PRACTICE

1 Choose a page of picture cards and make a copy for each child and one for the demonstration. Cut apart the cards in advance. Present one picture from each set of cards as the "key picture card." (See page 62 for a list of suggestions.) **Identify** the key picture name, and then say the target sound. For example, say: "*Mug…mmmug* begins with the /m/ sound" or "*Cat…caaat* ends with the sounds –*at.*"

2 Review the rest of the picture names with children. Emphasize the target sound in each word.

3 Model how to **sort** the cards. Start each category with the key picture card. Have children **compare** the target sound in each picture name to the target sound in the key picture card name. For example, tell children: "Listen for the beginning sound in each picture name and decide if it sounds like /m/ in *mmmug* or /s/ in *sssun.*"

4 Mix up the cards and have children **sort again** several times.

Tip For children with strong phonemic awareness skills, present a letter card that corresponds with the target sound.

SORT AGAIN/COLOR

1 Have children **recall** the target sounds that were introduced. Present each key picture card again to reinforce the key picture name.

2 Give children pre-cut picture cards and **review** each picture name.

3 Have children **color** the picture cards.

4 Invite children to **sort** the pictures independently or with partners. (This can also be done at learning centers.)

Tip Provide an envelope or large paper clip to store each child's picture cards.

DAY 3

DRAW

1 **Review** the target sounds with the whole group using the key picture cards. Have children sort additional cards that feature words with these sounds. (Draw or cut out pictures from old workbooks, catalogs, or magazines and paste them onto blank cards.)

2 Distribute crayons or markers along with index cards or copies of the blank cards on page 61. Have children **draw** pictures of objects whose names feature the target sounds.

3 Have children **sort** their new cards into categories. You might fold an 11- by 17-inch sheet of paper in half and have children paste a set of cards onto each half.

DAY 4

SEARCH FOR PICTURES

1 To **review**, present each key picture card again to help children associate the target sound with the picture name.

2 Extend Step 2 of Day 3 by having children **search** through old magazines and catalogs for additional pictures to cut out.

3 Have children **paste** the new pictures onto index cards or copies of the blank cards on page 61.

4 Invite children to **sort** their pictures into categories or add them to the pictures sorted in Step 3 of Day 3.

5 Encourage children to **search** for additional objects in your classroom whose names feature the target sounds. For reinforcement, point out appropriate words in picture books as you read aloud to the class.

DAY 5

GAMES

1 Follow up the week's activities by having partners or small groups **play** selected games on pages 52–60.

2 Model how to play the games for small groups. Leave the games at learning centers for children to play with partners.

3 Informally **assess** a few children each week by having them sort picture cards into two categories on their own.

Tip Observing how children sort will give you insights about their developmental level. Ask children to explain why they sorted the cards as they did.

9

Recognizing Rhymes

The ability to recognize rhyming words is an important form of phonological awareness. When children play with rhyme, they focus on the similarities and differences among words. By recognizing that two words rhyme, children shift gears from meaning to sound. Sensitivity to rhyme is a valuable step in developing phonological awareness.

This section includes 11 pages of reproducible cards. Each page features two sets of three rhyming picture cards. The section begins with obvious contrasts and progresses to finer ones. Each page may be used as a picture-sorting activity (see pages 4–9 for instructions) or you may extend learning by having children sort sets of cards from different pages.

Rhyming Assessment

Informally assess children's sensitivity to rhyme by saying two words that rhyme and one that does not. Ask children which two words rhyme. Then say a real or nonsense word and ask children to respond with a rhyming word.

Use the reproducible on page 11 to further assess children's ability to recognize rhyming words. Tell children: "Two words rhyme when they sound alike at the end. The words *hat* and *cat* rhyme. *Book* and *cook* rhyme. What words can you think of that rhyme with *hat*? What words rhyme with *book*? *big*? *car*?"

Give each child a copy of the reproducible. Now tell them: "Look at the pictures on the top of the page. Let's name the pictures together: *crown, shell, bug, king*. Now let's look at the pictures at the bottom of the page and name them: *rug, clown, ring, bell*."

Show children how to cut out the bottom row of pictures and then cut apart the four

picture cards. Explain to children that they will match each picture card with a picture whose name rhymes with it. Guide children as they paste the pictures in the blank spaces below the appropriate rhyming words.

Variations

✫ Show children a group of picture cards, and have them tell which one doesn't rhyme. Select two or three familiar pictures whose names rhyme and one picture whose name does not rhyme. Line up the cards in random order. Have children select the picture whose name does not rhyme with the others. Repeat, using different sets of cards. For example:

✫ For children who need further reinforcement, display only two picture cards. Ask if the picture names rhyme. Gradually increase the number of cards.

✫ For more of a challenge, mix up three pairs of picture cards whose names rhyme. Help children identify each picture. Then have them match the rhyming pairs. Challenge children to think of additional words that rhyme.

10

Rhyming Assessment

Rhyming Picture Cards

-at, -ice

bat, cat, hat, mice, dice, rice

Picture Sorting for Phonemic Awareness   Scholastic Professional Books

Rhyming Picture Cards

-ip, -ake

ship, chip, rip, snake, rake, cake

13

Rhyming Picture Cards

-ain, -ing

train, rain, chain, king, wing, ring

Picture Sorting for Phonemic Awareness Scholastic Professional Books

Rhyming Picture Cards

-ug, -ar

rug, mug, bug, car, jar, star

Rhyming Picture Cards

-ail, -in

nail, snail, tail, pin, chin, fin

Picture Sorting for Phonemic Awareness   Scholastic Professional Books

Rhyming Picture Cards

-ill, -og

grill, spill, pill, frog, log, dog

Rhyming Picture Cards

-ee, -oon

bee, knee, tree, spoon, balloon, moon

Rhyming Picture Cards

-an, -ate

fan, can, pan, gate, skate, plate

19

Rhyming Picture Cards

-aw, -ape

saw, straw, paw, grape, cape, tape

Rhyming Picture Cards

-en, -ell

Picture Sorting for Phonemic Awareness   Scholastic Professional Books

pen, hen, men, bell, well, shell

Rhyming Picture Cards

-ock, -op

clock, rock, lock, top, mop, stop

Picture Sorting for Phonemic Awareness Scholastic Professional Books

Matching Beginning Sounds

Recognizing and distinguishing initial sounds of words leads children to discover that words contain phonemes. The ability to match words that share the same beginning sound is a first and sometimes difficult step in the development of phonemic awareness. Initial sounds are easier for children to isolate than final or medial sounds.

Direct children's attention to how and where phonemes are articulated in the mouth since it is easier to feel the distinguishing characteristics of phonemes than it is to hear them. Suggest that they observe your mouth (or each other's) as you elongate phonemes. Ask children questions about the positions of the tongue, lips, and mouth when focusing on individual sounds in isolation.

This section includes 15 pages of reproducible cards. Each page features two sets of four picture cards that begin with the same sound. The last six pages include difficult initial sounds to contrast because they are articulated in the same place in the mouth. Each page may be used as a picture-sorting activity (see pages 4–9 for instructions) or you may extend learning by having children sort sets of cards from different pages.

Assessment

Informally assess children's ability to determine if words begin with the same sound. First say three words and ask which two begin with the same sound. Then say a word and ask children to respond with another word that begins with the same sound. Avoid words that begin with digraphs or blends, as well as polysyllabic words, so that children have fewer sounds to attend to. Hold up a book and tell children: "What is the first sound you hear in the word *book*? Yes, /b/, *bbbook*." Continue with other words that begin with single consonant sounds. Build children's confidence by working with a few sounds at a time.

Give each child a copy of the reproducible on page 24. Tell children: "Look at the pictures on the top of the page. Let's name the pictures together: *mop, carrot, watch, leaf.* Now let's look at the pictures at the bottom of the page and name them: *mitten, ladder, cake, wagon.*"

Show children how to cut out the bottom row of pictures and then cut apart the four picture cards. Explain to children that they will match each picture with a picture whose name begins with the same sound. Guide children as they paste each picture card in the blank space below its match.

Variations

⭐ Show children a group of picture cards and have them tell which one doesn't belong. Select two or three picture cards whose names have the same initial sound and one picture whose name has a different initial sound. Line up the cards in random order. Have children select the picture whose name does not begin with the same sound. Repeat, using different sets of cards. For example:

⭐ For children who need more help, display only two picture cards at a time. Ask if the picture names begin with the same sound. (Some pairs can begin with the same sound and some with different sounds.) Gradually increase the number of cards.

Beginning Sounds Assessment

/m/, /s/

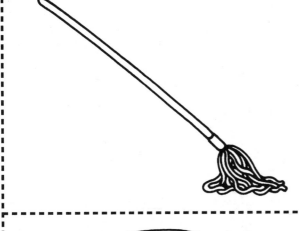

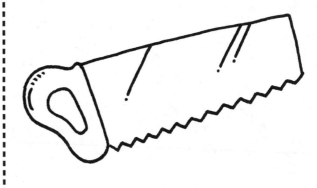

mop, mug, milk, mice, sun, sock, saw, soap

Beginning Sounds Picture Cards

/p/, /t/

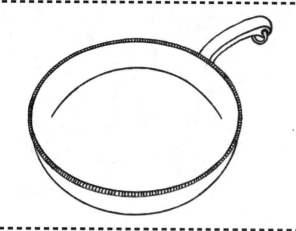

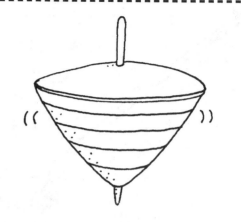

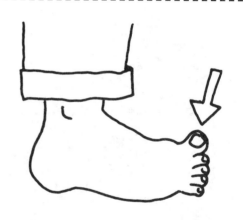

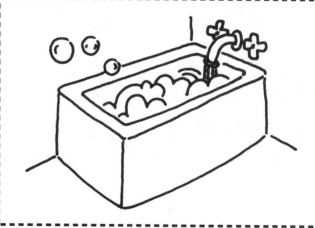

pan, pie, pen, pail, top, tent, toe, tub

Beginning Sounds Picture Cards

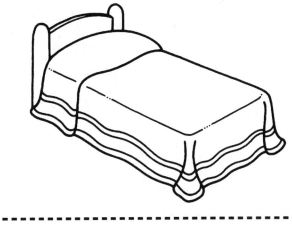

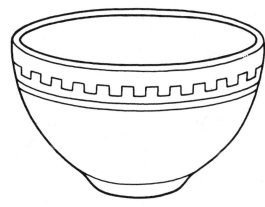

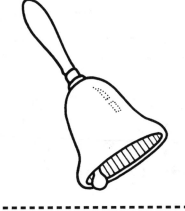

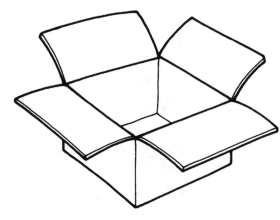

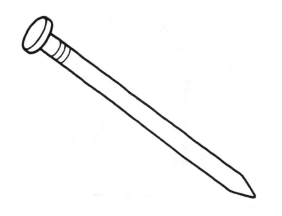

Picture Sorting for Phonemic Awareness   Scholastic Professional Books

bed, bowl, bell, box, nest, nut, nose, nail

Beginning Sounds Picture Cards

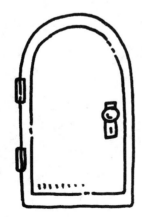

duck, doll, dog, door, gate, goat, game, girl

Picture Sorting for Phonemic Awareness   Scholastic Professional Books

Beginning Sounds Picture Cards

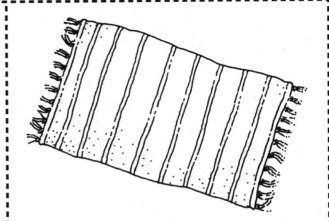

fish, fan, fox, fork, rug, rabbit, rake, rope

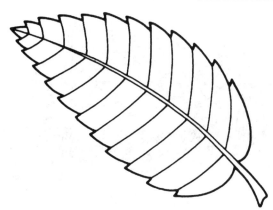

Picture Sorting for Phonemic Awareness   Scholastic Professional Books

lamp, log, lock, leaf, wagon, watch, well, worm

Beginning Sounds Picture Cards

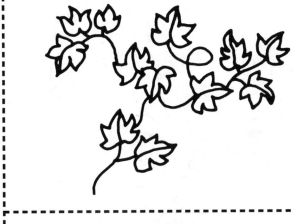

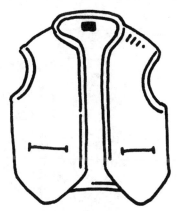

Picture Sorting for Phonemic Awareness   Scholastic Professional Books

vine, vest, vase, van, jar, jump, jug, jacks

31

Beginning Sounds Picture Cards

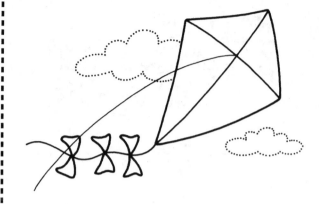

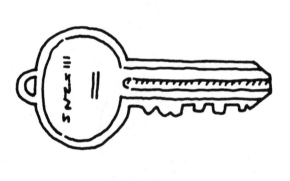

32

hat, heart, hen, house, kite, king, key, kitten

Beginning Sounds Picture Cards

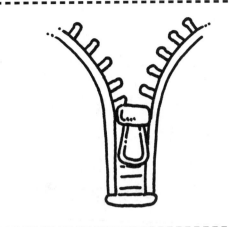

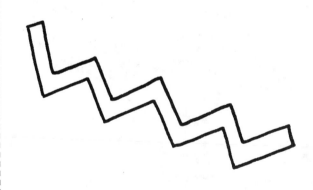

Picture Sorting for Phonemic Awareness   Scholastic Professional Books

zipper, zebra, zigzag, zoo, yarn, yard, yolk, yo-yo

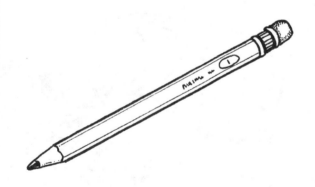

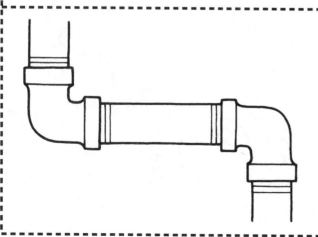

pig, pumpkin, pencil, pipe, ball, bike, bird, bag

Beginning Sounds Picture Cards

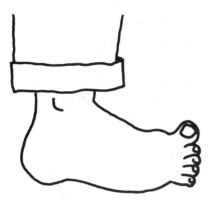

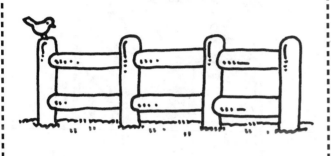

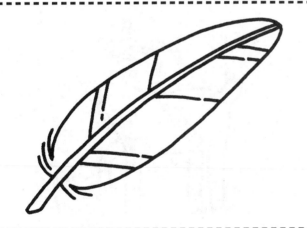

foot, fence, feather, fin, violin, volcano, vest, van

Beginning Sounds Picture Cards

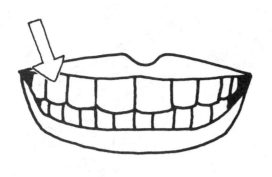

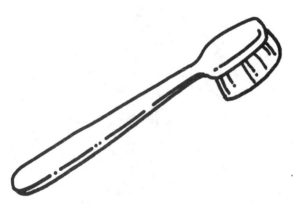

Picture Sorting for Phonemic Awareness   Scholastic Professional Books

teeth, tail, toothbrush, table, dice, desk, deer, dinosaur

Beginning Sounds Picture Cards

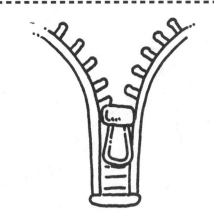

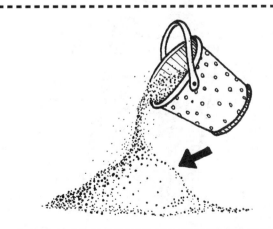

seal, sandwich, seed, sand, zipper, zebra, zigzag, zoo

Beginning Sounds Picture Cards

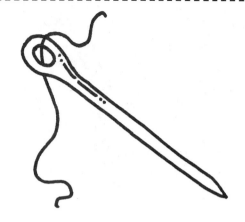

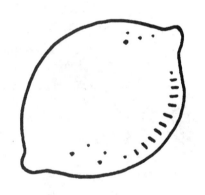

Picture Sorting for Phonemic Awareness   Scholastic Professional Books

needle, newspaper, napkin, net, lunch, lion, lemon, ladder

Beginning Sounds Picture Cards

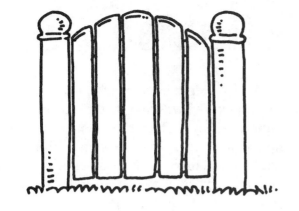

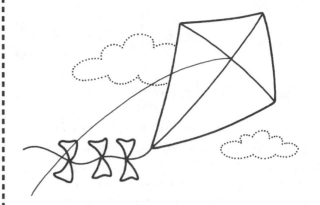

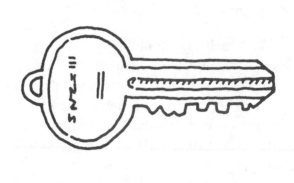

Picture Sorting for Phonemic Awareness   Scholastic Professional Books

gate, gum, guitar, game, kite, king, key, kitten

39

Counting Syllables

Once children are aware that sentences are composed of words, they are ready to learn that words are composed of syllables. Explain to children that syllables of spoken words can be heard and felt. Say several examples and point out how each syllable relates to the opening and closing of the jaw. Oral segmentation activities, such as counting syllables, help get children ready for spelling. When children spell words, they break them down into component sounds.

This section includes four pages of reproducible cards. The first three pages each include two sets of four cards. (Each set has the same number of syllables.) The last page includes four sets of two cards. Each page may be used as a picture-sorting activity (see pages 4–9 for instructions) or you may extend learning by having children sort sets of cards from different pages.

Assessment

Informally assess children's ability to break words into syllables. Have them clap the syllables in their own names and then count them. Demonstrate by clapping as you clearly enunciate each syllable in familiar two-syllable words such as: *rab-bit, flow-er, ta-ble*. Explain that each of these words has two parts, or syllables. Continue with other words, randomly saying one-, two-, three-, and even four-syllable words. Use words such as: *mys-ter-y, ap-ple, farm, li-brar-y, pump-kin, five, bi-cy-cle*. Have children repeat each word, clap out the syllables with you, and count how many syllables they hear.

Give each child a copy of the reproducible on page 41. Tell children: "Look at the numerals on the top of the page. Let's say them together: *1, 2, 3, 4*. Now let's look at the pictures at the bottom of the page and name them: *astronaut, tent, candles, caterpillar*."

Show children how to cut out the bottom row of picture cards and then cut apart the four cards. Say each picture name as you clap the number of syllables. Explain to children that they will place each card below the number of syllables they hear in the picture name. Guide children as they paste the picture cards in the appropriate blank spaces.

Variations

★ Have children say their names and stand in groups according to the number of syllables. Write their names on index cards and make numeral cards for 1–4. Place the numeral cards in the top row of a pocket chart. Challenge children to sort the names below the appropriate number of syllables.

★ Ask children to count the number of syllables in content-related vocabulary words. (Find pictures if possible.) Have them count the number of syllables in the names of objects around the classroom.

★ Place numeral cards for 1–4 in the top row of a pocket chart. Have children each select a picture card, say its name, and then clap and count the number of syllables. Children then place the card in the pocket chart below the corresponding number of syllables. Review the pictures in each column after all the cards have been sorted.

★ Once children are comfortable with counting syllables, challenge them to sort the cards by number of syllables *without* saying the picture word aloud and without clapping. Removing the kinesthetic aspect makes this a more challenging activity for many children.

Picture Sorting for Phonemic Awareness   Scholastic Professional Books

Counting Syllables Assessment

1	2	3	4

Counting Syllables Picture Cards

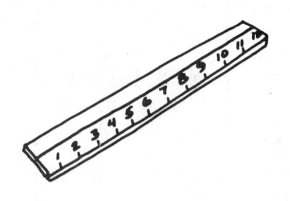

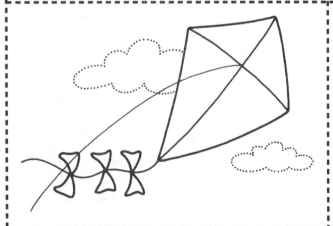

duck, book, kite, cow, ruler, zebra, snowman, ladder

Picture Sorting for Phonemic Awareness   Scholastic Professional Books

Counting Syllables Picture Cards

2 and 3 Syllables

Picture Sorting for Phonemic Awareness   Scholastic Professional Books

carrot, rabbit, turkey, mitten, kangaroo, banana, octopus, strawberry

Counting Syllables Picture Cards

elephant, umbrella, butterfly, violin, alligator, watermelon, television, motorcycle

Counting Syllables Picture Cards

cake, dog, pencil, balloon, newspaper, piano, rhinoceros, helicopter

Counting Phonemes

To learn sound–letter correspondences (phonics), children must become aware of phonemes. Although awareness of phonemes is a strong predictor of reading achievement, counting phonemes is extremely challenging for some children. Children have more difficulty conceptualizing phonemes than syllables or words because phonemes in isolation have no meaning.

Phonemes cannot be distinguished very easily in spoken words, and they sound different depending on the word and speaker. Phonemes can be most easily distinguished by how they are articulated. Provide small, unbreakable mirrors, if available, and have children study their mouth and tongue positions as they say individual sounds. Have children observe you and one another while saying various words and emphasizing each sound.

Assessment

Informally assess children's ability to count phonemes by saying a word and asking how many different sounds they hear. Indicate each sound using tally marks on the chalkboard or a different color block, arranged from left to right. Invite children to use blocks or other tangible objects to represent the number of individual phonemes in a word.

Say the word *hi* and then slowly repeat the word: "*H-h-h-i-i-i.*" Ask children: "What is the first sound you hear in *hi*? Yes, you hear /h/. Then what do you hear?" Demonstrate the long *i* sound. Ask children how many sounds they hear in the word *hi*. Again, demonstrate both sounds separately. Then say: "To show that *hi* has two sounds, I am making a mark on the chalkboard (or, I am placing a colored block) as I say each sound." Continue in the same way with additional words that are made up of two or three sounds, such as *day* (2), *head* (3), and *coat* (3).

Give each child a copy of the reproducible on page 47. Tell children: "Look at the numerals on the top of the page. Let's say them together: *2, 3, 4.* Now let's look at the pictures at the bottom of the page and name them: *boots, bee, pan.*"

Show children how to cut out the bottom row of pictures and then cut apart the three picture cards. Say each picture name and count the number of separate sounds. Explain to children that they will place each picture card below the number of sounds they hear in its name. Guide children as they paste the pictures in the blank spaces below the appropriate numerals.

Variations

☆ Use additional picture cards. Have children sort them into two or three categories according to the number of phonemes in each picture word (two, three, and/or four). Additional picture words with two phonemes include: *ape, hay, pea,* and *tea.* Additional picture words with three phonemes include *cup, bus, dog,* and *cat.*

☆ Display two pictures or objects for children to name. Invite them to choose the one whose name is longer or has more sounds.

☆ Invite pairs or small groups of children to search for pictures with a specified number of phonemes. Have them cut out pictures from old magazines and catalogs and share them with other groups.

Picture Sorting for Phonemic Awareness   Scholastic Professional Books

Counting Phonemes Assessment

2	3	4

Counting Phonemes Picture Cards

2 and 3 Phonemes

knee, egg, pie, bed, pig, tub

Counting Phonemes Picture Cards

2 and 3 Phonemes

tie, zoo, key, dice, mug, bell

Counting Phonemes Picture Cards

2 and 3 Phonemes

ice, hay, toe, kite, soap, rake

Picture Sorting for Phonemic Awareness   Scholastic Professional Books

Counting Phonemes Picture Cards

3 and 4 Phonemes

pen, moon, lock, tent, cats, socks

Picture-Sorting Games and Activities

Clothespin Match

(2 players)

SETUP

Chose two to three target sounds (or features) you would like children to review, and find a key picture card for each sound. Clip a clothespin to each picture card. Provide additional picture cards that feature the target sounds.

TO PLAY

1 Shuffle the picture cards and place them facedown in a pile.

2 Each player, in turn, picks the top card and says the picture name. The player clips the card in the clothespin with the picture that features the same target sound.

3 When the entire pile is sorted, have children say the names of each group of cards clipped together.

VARIATION . . . .

Include some cards that do not fit into any category.

. . . .

Concentration

(2 players)

SETUP

Determine if children will practice identifying rhyming words, beginning sounds, number of syllables, or number of phonemes. Provide four to six pairs of picture cards with target sounds or features that children have reviewed. You may include more than one pair of cards with the same sound or feature.

TO PLAY

1 Shuffle the cards and place them facedown in rows of an equal number.

2 Players take turns turning over two cards to make a match between the picture names. (For example, the picture names rhyme or have the same number of syllables.)

3 If the cards match, the player removes the two cards and takes another turn. If the cards do not match, the player returns both cards facedown to their original positions.

4 The game continues until no cards remain or no additional matches can be made.

What's My Category?

(2 players)

SETUP

Photocopy three to four sets of matching cards, such as *snake*, *rake*, and *cake* (9 to 16 cards all together). Choose sets of cards from different sections of the book. This game allows children to practice open sorts (sorting cards into categories of their own choosing rather than categories specified by the teacher).

TO PLAY

1 Shuffle the cards and place them faceup in equal rows.

2 Player 1 selects a card, says the picture name, and places the card apart from the other cards.

3 Player 2 selects a matching card (a card with a picture name that rhymes, begins with the same sound, or contains the same number of syllables or phonemes). Player 2 says the picture name and places it with its match.

4 Player 1 selects a third card that matches and places it with the other two cards.

5 Players take turns finding cards that fit into the same category. When a player cannot find any more cards that fit into the category, the player selects a card that belongs in a different category. Play continues in the same way until there are no cards left. Some categories might have only one card.

6 At the end of the game, players say the picture names of the cards in each category.

Picture Sorting for Phonemic Awareness   Scholastic Professional Books

Go Fish

(2 players)

SETUP

Make copies of the Go Fish cards on page 55. Determine if you would like children to practice identifying rhyming words, beginning sounds, number of syllables, or number of phonemes. Cut out picture cards for three related words (such as *snake*, *rake*, and *cake*) and paste them onto "fish" cards. Make three or more sets of fish cards with related words, depending on players' skill levels. Laminate the cards for greater durability. The object of the game is to obtain three matching cards (rhyming, same beginning sound, and so on).

TO PLAY

1 Shuffle the cards and deal three cards to each player. Place the remaining cards facedown in a pile.

2 Players check their hand for three matching picture cards. If a player has a set of matching cards, he or she says the picture names and places the cards on the table.

3 If neither player has a matching set, Player 1 asks Player 2 for a card that matches with one she or he is holding. (For example: "Do you have a card that rhymes with *cat*?")

4 If Player 2 has a matching card, he or she gives it to Player 1, and Player 1 takes another turn. If Player 2 does not have a matching card, he or she says, "Go fish," and Player 1 draws the top card from the pile. If Player 1 is able to make a match, he or she takes another turn. Otherwise, Player 2 takes a turn.

5 The first player to obtain three matching cards wins.

Dominoes

(2 players)

SETUP

Photocopy three to four sets of matching cards, such as *snake*, *rake*, and *cake* (9 to 16 cards all together). Choose sets of cards from different sections of the book.

TO PLAY

1 Shuffle the cards and place them faceup in equal rows.

2 Player 1 selects a card, says the picture name, and places the card apart from the other cards.

3 Player 2 selects a card that shares a common feature with the first card (rhymes, begins with the same sound, or has the same number of syllables or phonemes). Player 2 says the picture name, explains how the cards match, and places it beside its matching card.

4 Player 1 selects a card that shares a common feature with the second card. The common feature can be the same as the first match or it can be different. The player says the picture name and explains how the cards match.

5 Play continues in the same way until no cards remain or no additional matches can be made.

Reach the Top

(2 players)

SETUP

Photocopy the two halves of the game board on pages 56–57 and tape them together. You might paste the game board in a file folder or laminate for greater durability. Determine if you would like children to practice identifying rhyming words, beginning sounds, number of syllables, or number of phonemes. Choose a target sound or feature you would like children to review and find a key picture card. Tape the key picture card in the box at the top of the board.

Photocopy one to two sets of picture cards that feature the target sound and one to two sets of picture cards that do not. Provide a number cube (page 60) and playing pieces (such as colored paper clips, plastic figures, or different shaped pasta noodles).

TO PLAY

1 Shuffle the picture cards and place them facedown in a pile.

2 In turn, each player rolls the number cube and moves ahead that number of spaces.

3 The player selects the top card and says the picture name. If the picture name features the target sound or feature, the player moves ahead two spaces. Otherwise the player remains in the same space. The player returns the card to the bottom of the pile.

4 The first player to reach Finish wins.

VARIATION . . . .

To give children practice counting syllables or phonemes, write *1, 2, 3,* and *4* in the spaces on the game board. In the last space, write *1, 2, 3,* or *4.* Provide four sets of picture cards from the counting syllables section or counting phonemes section. To take a turn, a player picks the top card from the pile, says the picture name, and counts the number of syllables or phonemes. The player then moves his or her playing piece to the next space that shows the same number.

. . . .

Blast Off!

(2 players)

SETUP

Photocopy the two halves of the game board on pages 58–59 and tape them together. Determine if you would like children to practice identifying rhyming words, beginning sounds, number of syllables, or number of phonemes. Photocopy 14 picture cards from various sets within one section of the book. Cut out the cards and tape them in random order in the spaces on the board. Photocopy the rocket

playing pieces below, cut them out, and color them each a different color. Provide a number cube (page 60).

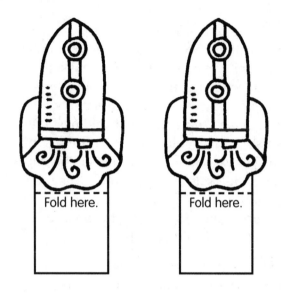

Fold here.   Fold here.

TO PLAY

1 Players place their pieces in the Start space.

2 To take a turn, a player rolls the number cube and moves ahead that number of spaces.

3 The player lands on a picture and says the picture name. The player then thinks of a word that matches (rhymes, has the same beginning sound, number of syllables, or number of phonemes—depending on what you determined when creating the board). For a challenge, players think of two matching words.

4 The first player to reach the moon wins.

Go Fish Cards

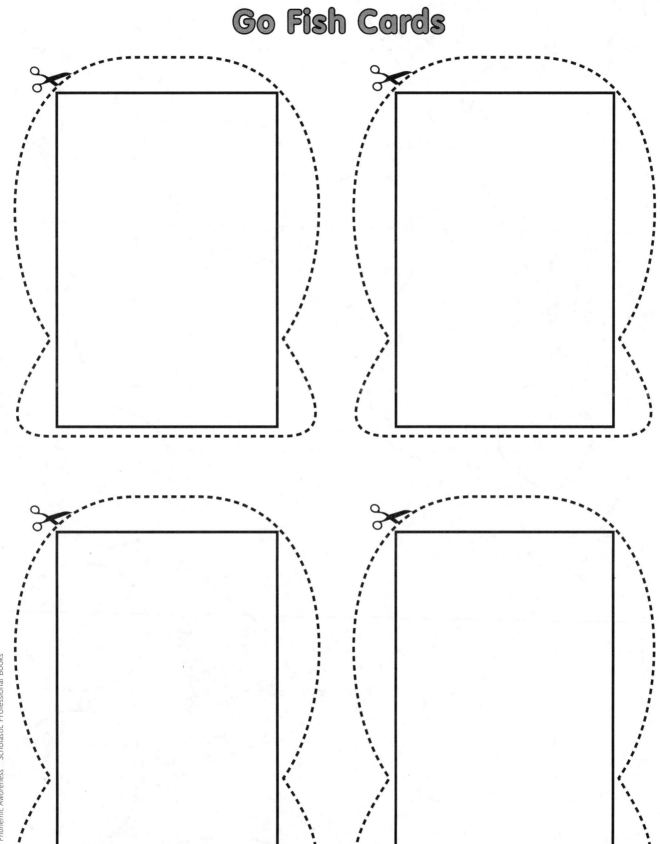

Reach-the-Top Game Board

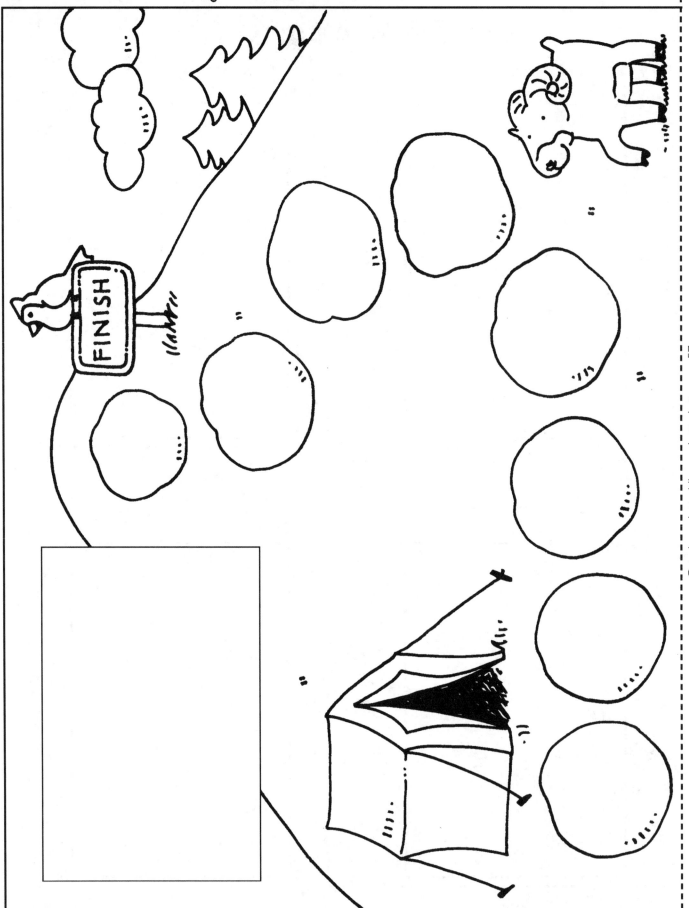

FINISH

Attach to page 56 here.

Blast Off! Game Board

Start

Picture Sorting for Phonemic Awareness Scholastic Professional Books

Cut along dotted line and attach to page 59.

Finish

Number Cubes

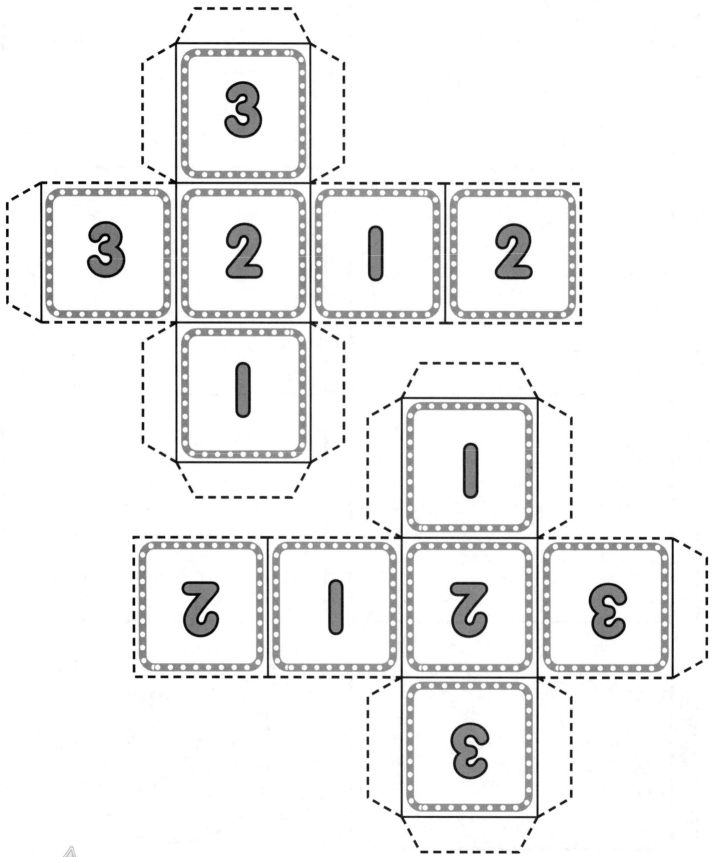

Picture Cards Template

Picture Sorting for Phonemic Awareness   Scholastic Professional Books

Word Lists

KEY PICTURE CARDS

page 12: cat, mice
page 13: rip, cake
page 14: rain, king
page 15: bug, car
page 16: nail, fin
page 17: pill, dog
page 18: bee, moon
page 19: can, gate
page 20: saw, tape
page 21: hen, bell
page 22: lock, mop
page 25: mug, sun
page 26: pan, tub
page 27: box, nest
page 28: duck, gate,
page 29: fish, rug
page 30: lamp, wagon
page 31: vest, jug
page 32: hat, kite
page 33: zipper, yarn
page 34: pig, ball
page 35: foot, vest
page 36: tail, desk
page 37: seed, zipper
page 38: net, lion
page 39: gate, kite

ADDITIONAL PICTURE WORDS

ant	dig	kettle	sailboat
apple	dime	kitchen	scarf
ax	dish	leg	school
baby	dive	leash	sheep
backpack	dock	lip	shelf
barn	dress	lunchbox	shirt
baseball	drum	mail	shoe
basket	elbow	mailbox	shovel
beach	envelope	man	skirt
beak	farm	map	slide
bear	feet	marbles	spider
belt	finger	mask	tack
bench	flashlight	mat	telephone
bib	flower	mirror	tiger
block	flute	monkey	tire
boat	fly	mouse	tomato
bone	football	mouth	towel
bottle	frown	mushroom	truck
bow	fruit	neck	trunk
boy	garden	necklace	turtle
bread	gold	nickel	valentine
bridge	goose	nurse	wand
bus	gorilla	paint	wave
button	grass	pea	web
cage	hair	peach	wig
camel	ham	pear	window
camera	hammer	penguin	yawn
cane	hand	penny	yak
cap	head	pickle	yardstick
cave	heel	pillow	yogurt
chair	hill	plant	zip
cheese	hive	pot	
cherry	hole	puppet	
chest	horse	purse	
chimney	hose	puzzle	
circle	hug	radio	
coat	ink	rainbow	
coins	jacket	ram	
comb	jail	road	
cone	jam	robe	
corn	jeans	rocket	
crab	jeep	roof	
cube	jump rope	run	
cup	ketchup	safe	

Picture Sorting for Phonemic Awareness   Scholastic Professional Books

Read-Aloud Books

All About You by Catherine and Laurence Anholt (Puffin, 1994)

Barnyard Banter by Denise Fleming (Henry Holt, 2001)

Buzz Said the Bee by Wendy Cheyette Lewison (Scholastic, 1992)

The Cat Barked? by Lydia Monks (Puffin, 2001)

Chicka Chicka Boom Boom by Bill Martin, Jr. and John Archambault (Simon & Schuster, 1992)

Chicken Soup With Rice by Maurice Sendak (Harper & Row, 1962)

Chugga-Chugga Choo-Choo by Kevin Lewis (Hyperion Press, 1999)

Cock-a-doodle-do! Barnyard Hullabaloo by Giles Andreae (Tiger Tales, 2002)

Commotion in the Ocean by Giles Andreae (Tiger Tales, 2001)

Cows Can't Fly by David Milgrim (Viking, 1998)

Dinosaur Roar! by Paul and Henrietta Strickland (Puffin, 2002)

Dr. Seuss's ABC by Dr. Seuss (Random House, 1963)

Engine, Engine, Number Nine by Stephanie Calmenson (Disney Press, 1997)

Fathers, Mothers, Sisters, Brothers by Mary Ann Hoberman (Little, Brown, 2001)

Five Little Monkeys Jumping on the Bed retold by Eileen Christelow (Houghton Mifflin, 1998)

Gifts by Jo Ellen Bogart and Barbara Reid (Scholastic, 1995)

Hey, Little Ant by Phillip and Hannah Hoose (Tricycle Press, 1998)

"I Can't," Said the Ant by Polly Cameron (Putnam, 1961)

I Love You: A Rebus Poem by Jean Marzollo (Scholastic, 2000)

Is Your Mama a Llama? by Deborah Guarino (Scholastic, 1991)

Itchy, Itchy Chicken Pox by Grace Maccarone (Scholastic, 1992)

I Was Walking Down the Road by Sarah E. Barchas (Scholastic, 1993)

Jamberry by Bruce Degan (Harper & Row, 1985)

Madeline by Ludwig Bemelmans (Viking, 1958)

Mice Squeak, We Speak by Tomie dePaola and Arnold L. Shapiro (Putnam, 2002)

Millions of Snowflakes by Mary McKenna Siddals (Clarion, 1998)

Miss Mary Mack and Other Children's Street Rhymes by Joanna Cole and Stephanie Calmenson (Morrow, 1990)

Mrs. McNosh Hangs Up Her Wash by Sarah Weeks (HarperCollins, 1998)

The New Kid on the Block by Jack Prelutsky (Scholastic, 1987)

Over in the Meadow by David A. Carter (Scholastic, 1992)

Pass It On: African-American Poetry for Children selected by Wade Hudson (Scholastic, 1993)

Pigs in the Mud in the Middle of the Rud by Lynn Plourde (Scholastic, 1997)

Play Rhymes by Marc Brown (Dutton, 1987)

Sheep in a Jeep by Nancy Shaw (Houghton Mifflin, 1986)

Silly Sally by Audrey Wood (Harcourt, 1992)

Sing a Song of Popcorn by Beatrice Schenk de Regniers, E. Moore, M. White, and J. Carr (Scholastic, 1988)

Sometimes I Wonder if Poodles Like Noodles by Laura Numeroff (Simon & Schuster, 1999)

Splish Splash by Joan Bransfield Graham (Ticknor & Fields, 1994)

There Was an Old Lady Who Swallowed a Fly by Simms Taback (Viking, 1997)

Three Little Kittens by Lorianne Siomades (Boyds Mills Press, 2000)

Time for Bed by Mem Fox (Red Wagon, 1997)

To Market, To Market by Anne Miranda (Voyager, 2001)

Tumble Bumble by Felicia Bond (Front Street, 1996)

Bibliography

Adams, Marilyn Jager. *Beginning to Read: Thinking and Learning About Print.* Cambridge, MA: The MIT Press, 1995.

Adams, Marilyn, Barbara R. Foorman, Ingvar Lundberg, and Terri Beeler. *Phonemic Awareness in Young Children: A Classroom Curriculum.* Baltimore: Paul H. Brookes Publishing Co., 1998.

Baker, Linda, Miriam Jean Dreher, and John T. Guthrie. *Engaging Young Readers: Promoting Achievement and Motivation.* New York: The Guilford Press, 2000.

Bear, Donald R., Marcia Invernizzi, Shane Templeton, and Francine Johnston. *Words Their Way: Word Study for Phonics, Vocabulary, and Spelling Instruction.* Upper Saddle River, NJ: Merrill, 2000.

Blevins, Wiley. *Phonemic Awareness Activities for Early Reading Success.* New York: Scholastic, 1997.

Blevins, Wiley. *Phonics From A to Z: A Practical Guide.* New York: Scholastic, 1998.

Fountas, Irene C. and Gay Su Pinnell. *Guided Reading: Good First Teaching for All Children.* Portsmouth, NH: Heinemann, 1996.

Fountas, Irene C. and Gay Su Pinnell. *Guiding Readers and Writers.* Portsmouth, NH: Heinemann, 2000.

Honig, Bill. *How Should We Teach Our Children to Read?* San Francisco: Far West Laboratory for Educational Research and Development, 1996.

Moats, Louisa Cook. *Spelling: Development, Disabilities and Instruction.* Baltimore: York Press, 1995.

Moats, Louisa and John Shefelbine. *Phonemic Awareness: Teacher's Guide* (for Phonemic Awareness Kit). New York: Scholastic, 1997.

National Institute for Literacy. *Put Reading First.* Jessup, MD: U.S. Department of Education, 2001.

Rayner, Keith, Barbara R. Foorman, Charles A. Perfetti, David Pesetsky, and Mark S. Seidenberg. "How Should Reading Be Taught?" *Scientific American,* March 2002, 84–91.

Snow, Catherine E., M. Susan Burns, and Peg Griffin. *Preventing Reading Difficulties in Young Children.* Washington, D.C.: National Academy Press, 1998.